By Mary Holland

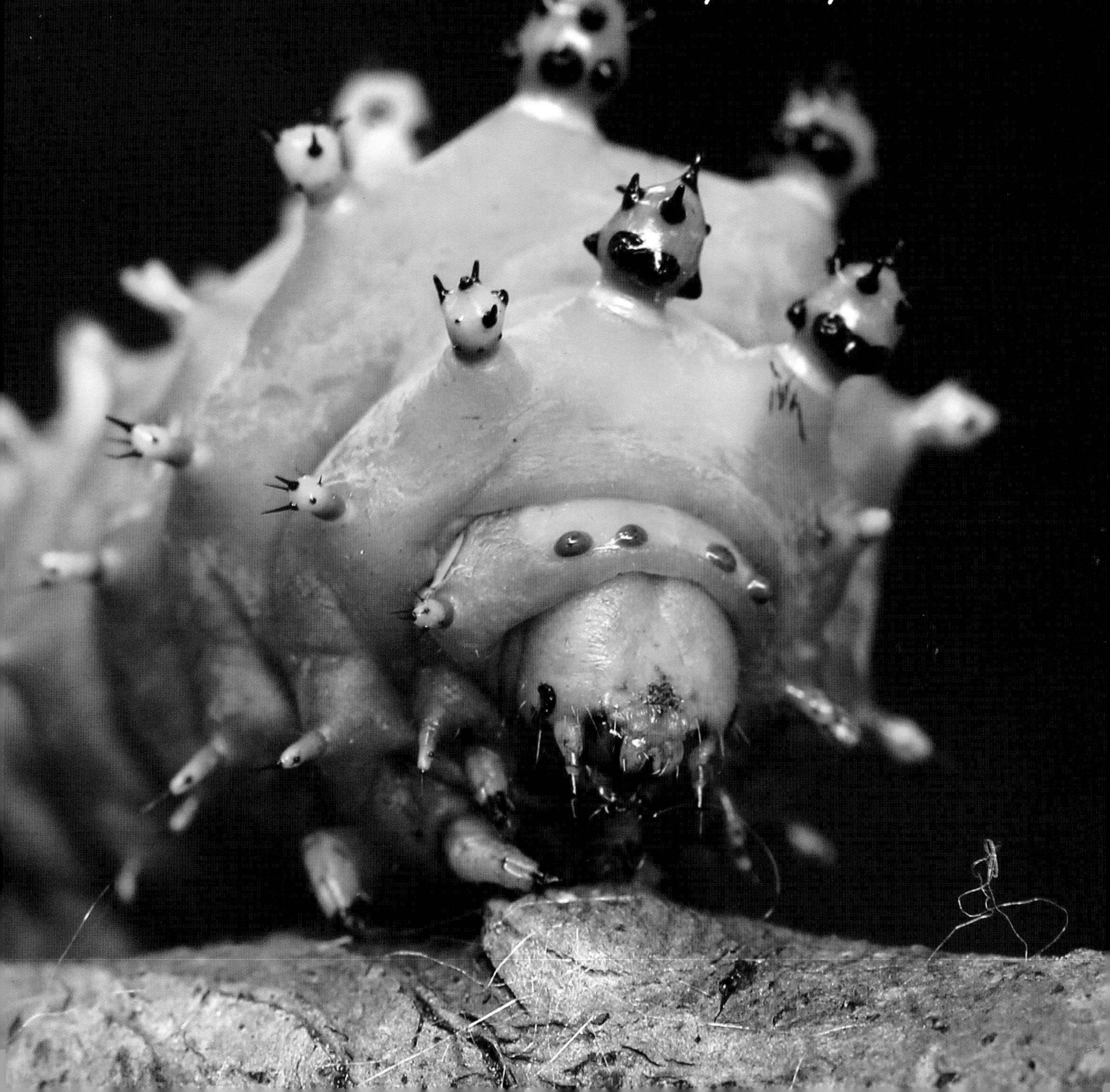

Most, but not all, animals have mouths. As a caterpillar, this luna moth had chewing mouthparts that it used to eat leaves. An adult luna moth doesn't have a mouth. Because luna moths only live for about a week, they don't need to eat!

Animals with mouths usually have teeth, but not always. Turtles don't have teeth. They use the sharp edges of their jaws to eat both plants and animals.

Birds have beaks instead of teeth. Beaks come in all different shapes and sizes, depending on what the birds eat. Evening grosbeaks have large, strong beaks for cracking seeds.

Eagles and hawks—like this red-shouldered hawk—have strong, curved beaks to tear the flesh of the animals they eat (prey).

Many birds that eat fish, frogs and other animals that live in the water have long, pointed beaks to grab their prey. This great egret caught a crayfish with its beak.

Most frogs have a row of very small teeth along the edge of their upper jaws and on the roof of their mouths. They use these teeth to hold onto insects, earthworms, and other food that they catch with their sticky tongue. Most frogs don't have any teeth on their lower jaw. This makes it hard to chew their food so they usually swallow prey whole.

Most snakes have teeth, but only venomous snakes have special teeth (fangs) that inject venom. If a snake breaks a tooth, it grows a new one to replace the broken tooth. A snake's sharp teeth help it hold onto mice and other animals that it eats. Like frogs, snakes don't chew their prey. They swallow it whole. Because they can stretch their jaw and open it wider than their body, they can eat very large prey.

Insects don't have teeth. They have many different kinds of mouthparts for eating different kinds of food.

Moths and butterflies—like this monarch—have long, hollow mouthparts that form a tube called a proboscis. Their proboscis is usually curled up until they land on a flower. Then they uncurl it and use it as a straw to drink a sweet liquid (nectar) that many flowers make.

Robber flies eat other insects. They use their hairy legs to catch an insect and then puncture the insect with their beaks. The robber flies' saliva turns the insides of the insects into a liquid. The flies use their piercing-sucking mouthparts to drink the insides of their prey.

Animals that eat plants are called herbivores. All herbivores—including deer, rabbits and moose—have flat teeth (molars) in the back of their mouths. These teeth grind up the plants for easy swallowing.

Some herbivores—including porcupines, mice, squirrels, woodchucks and beavers—are in the rodent family. All rodents have four large, sharp teeth in the front of their mouths (two in the upper jaw and two in the lower jaw). These teeth are called incisors and they never stop growing. Rodents like this porcupine keep them from getting too long by using them to cut leaves and gnaw bark.

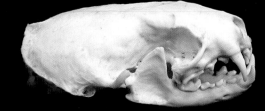

Animals that eat other animals are called carnivores. Many of their teeth are sharp and pointed to cut and tear the flesh of the animals they eat.

Four of these sharp teeth are called canines. In addition to their large canine teeth, some carnivores have carnassial teeth. These four, special teeth have edges as sharp as knives.

When this long-tailed weasel closes its jaw, the carnassial teeth slice past one another like scissor blades. This cuts the prey into pieces for the weasel to swallow.

Animals that eat both plants and animals are called omnivores. They usually have some flat teeth like plant eaters, and some sharp teeth like meat eaters.

Opossums are omnivores and will eat just about anything—plants, animals, and even garbage. They have 50 teeth—more than any other mammal in North America.

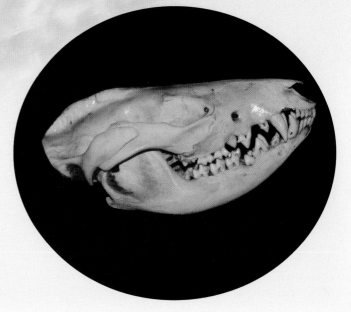

Most humans eat plants and animals, which makes us omnivores. Like the opossum, we have many different kinds of teeth. How many kinds can you find when you open your mouth and look in the mirror?

For Creative Minds

This For Creative Minds educational section contains activities to engage children in learning while making it fun at the same time. The activities build on the underlying subjects introduced in the story. While older children may be able to do these activities on their own, we encourage adults to work with the young children in their lives. Even if the adults have long forgotten or never learned this information, they can still work through the activities and be experts in their children's eyes! Exposure to these concepts at a young age helps to build a strong foundation for easier comprehension later in life. This section may be photocopied or printed from our website by the owner of this book for educational, non-commercial uses. Cross-curricular teaching activities for use at home or in the classroom, interactive quizzes, and more are available online. Go to www.ArbordalePublishing.com and click on the book's cover to explore all the links.

Mouths: Other Uses

Animal mouths are not just for eating! Animals use their mouths to communicate with other animals, to camouflage themselves, to yawn, to carry things, or to clean themselves.

Mammal Teeth

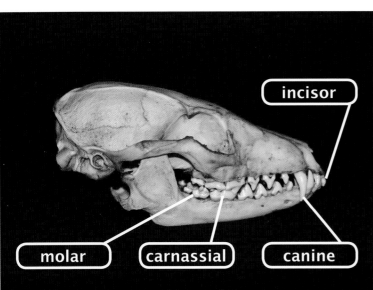

incisor

molar

carnassial

canine

A mammal's teeth can tell you what kind of food it eats. This is because teeth have different shapes for eating different foods.

Herbivores have teeth shaped for cutting and chewing plants (incisors and molars). Carnivores have teeth shaped for tearing and slicing meat (canines and carnassial teeth). Omnivores, like this red fox, can have many different kinds of teeth located at different places in their jaw.

1.
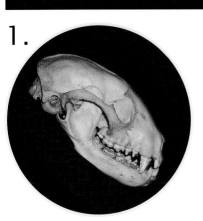

2.
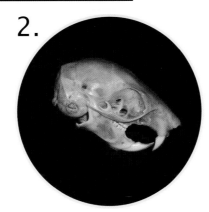

3.
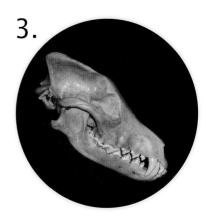

Can you match the photo of the skull to the animal?

red squirrel

coyote

raccoon

Answers: 1-raccoon. 2-red squirrel. 3-coyote

Bird Beaks

Just as mammals' teeth give us clues as to what the mammals eat, the shapes and sizes of birds' beaks tell us what they eat too. Read the descriptions for clues to match the beaks to the bird's prey. Answers are below.

1.

Common loons have long, pointed beaks for grasping slippery prey they find in the water.

A.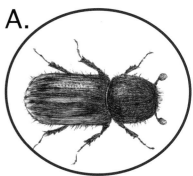

2.

American kestrels have strong, curved beaks that they use to tear up their prey into smaller pieces.

B.

3.

A ruby-throated hummingbird's long beak can fit into narrow places where they often get a sweet drink of nectar.

C.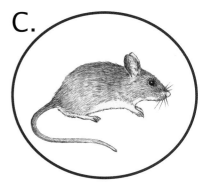

4.

Brown creepers have thin, curved beaks that are good for fitting under loose bark where they look for insects to eat.

D.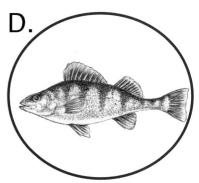

Answers: 1-D, 2-C, 3-B, 4-A.

Glossary

bird

insect

mammal

beak	a protruding, horny jaw of an animal
bird	an animal with feathers
canine	a long, pointed tooth (sometimes called a fang in mammals)
carnassial	a large tooth found in many carnivores that is adapted for cutting food
fang	a long, pointed tooth that injects venom
groom	to clean and arrange fur or feathers
incisor	a tooth in the front of the jaw that has a sharp edge for cutting food
inject	to force a liquid into something
insect	a small animal with three body sections, six legs, two antennae and no backbone (spine)
jaw	the bones that form the structure of the mouth and often hold teeth. The lower jaw (mandible) moves, allowing the animal to open and close its mouth. The upper jaw (maxilla) is part of the skull and does not move.
mammal	a warm-blooded animal with a spine, fur, and the ability to produce milk
molar	a large, flat tooth in the back of the jaw that is used for grinding food
mouth	the opening in the body through which an animal takes in food
preen	to smooth, clean or apply oil to feathers
proboscis	a hollow tube-like mouthpart that some insects use to suck or to pierce and suck
skull	the bones in the head that surround and protect the brain

To Mary Sue, who with great patience refined my photographic skills.—MH
Heartfelt thanks to Chiho Kaneko, whose beautiful illustrations enhance this book.

Thanks to Bill Creasey, Chief Naturalist for the Cincinnati Nature Center, for reviewing the accuracy of the information in this book.

Library of Congress Cataloging-in-Publication Data

Holland, Mary, 1946-
 Animal mouths / by Mary Holland.
    pages cm
 ISBN 978-1-62855-552-3 (English hardcover) -- ISBN 978-1-62855-561-5 (English pbk.) -- ISBN 978-1-62855-579-0 (English downloadable ebook) -- ISBN 978-1-62855-597-4 (English interactive dual-language ebook) -- ISBN 978-1-62855-570-7 (Spanish pbk.) -- ISBN 978-1-62855-588-2 (Spanish downloadable ebook) -- ISBN 978-1-62855-606-3 (Spanish interactive dual-language ebook) 1. Mouth--Juvenile literature. I. Title.
 QL857.H65 2015
 591.4'4--dc23
                    2014037325

Translated into Spanish: *Bocas de animales*

Lexile® Level: 920L
key phrases for educators: adaptations, carnivore, herbivore, mouths, omnivore, predator, prey, teeth

Bibliography:
"Mouthparts." Amateur Entomologists' Society. Web. Accessed July 2014.
Chapman, R.F. and Simpson, S.J. The Insects: Structure and Function. Cambridge University Press. 5th Edition, 2012. Print.
Elbroch, Mark. Animal Skulls: A Guide to North American Species. Stackpole Books, 2006. Print.
Proctor, Noble and Lynch, Patrick. Manual of Ornithology: Avian Structure and Function. Yale University Press, 1998. Print.

Manufactured in China, January, 2015
This product conforms to CPSIA 2008
First Printing

Arbordale Publishing
Mt. Pleasant, SC 29464
www.ArbordalePublishing.com